SCATALOG
A Kid's Field Guide to Animal Poop

HOW TO TRACK
A LEOPARD

Dory Zane

"BECAUSE EVERYBODY POOPS"

WINDMILL
BOOKS

New York

Published in 2014 by Windmill Books, An Imprint of Rosen Publishing
29 East 21st Street, New York, NY 10010

First Edition

Editor: Amelie von Zumbusch
Photo Research: Katie Stryker
Book Design: Colleen Bialecki

Photo Credits: Cover (top) Daleen Loest/Shutterstock.com; cover (bottom) Bob Hawley/Flickr; background iStockphoto/Thinkstock; p. 4 Sue Green/Shutterstock.com; pp. 5, 19 Jeannie Hayward & Anita Meyer, The Cape Leopard Trust Boland Project; p. 7 Keith Levit/Shutterstock.com; p. 8 Volodymyr Burdiak/ Shutterstock.com; pp. 9, 14, 22 EcoPrint/Shutterstock.com; p. 10 Leslie Crookes/Shutterstock.com; p. 11 Ingram Publishing/Thinkstock; p. 13 Stu Porter/Shutterstock.com; p. 15 Photodisc/Thinkstock; p. 17 pixelpics/Shutterstock.com;p. 18 Heinrich van den Berg/Getty Images; p. 19 (top left) Alexander Gilliland/Flickr; p. 21 Denis-Huot/Hemis.fr/Getty Images.

Library of Congress Cataloging-in-Publication Data

Zane, Dory.
 How to track a leopard / by Dory Zane. — First edition.
     pages cm. — (Scatalog: a kid's field guide to animal poop)
Includes index.
ISBN 978-1-61533-885-6 (library) — ISBN 978-1-61533-891-7 (pbk.) —
ISBN 978-1-61533-897-9 (6-pack)
1. Leopard—Juvenile literature. 2. Animal droppings—Juvenile literature. I. Title.
QL737.C23Z365 2014
599.75'54—dc23
                              2013023786

Manufactured in the United States of America

CPSIA Compliance Information: Batch # BW14WM: For Further Information contact Windmill Books, New York, New York at 1-866-478-0556

CONTENTS

Finding Leopard Poop 4

Where Leopards Live.................................... 6

Seeing Spots 8

In Leopard Territory 10

Look, It's a Cub! 12

Hunting Prey 14

What Leopards Eat 16

Tracking Methods.................................... 18

Leopards and People 20

Keeping Leopards Safe 22

Glossary.................................... 23

Index 24

Websites 24

FINDING LEOPARD POOP

Leopards are spotted big cats. They live in parts of Africa and Asia. Leopards can be hard to spot in the wild! They spend most of the day resting. Leopards often rest in tall grasses or high up in tree branches. Their spots help them blend in with their **habitats**.

Leopards are related to jaguars, lions, and tigers. These animals are the four kinds of big cats. Leopards are the smallest of the big cats.

LEOPARD POOP

Bone

Hoof or nail

Hair

Segment

Leopard poop looks a bit like the poop of other wild cats. However, it tends to be smaller than lion poop and bigger than caracal poop.

How do people learn about leopards if they are so hard to find? There are several ways to track leopards and other wild animals. One way is to find their poop, or scat. Tracking poop helps people learn what leopards have been eating and where their **territories** are.

WHERE LEOPARDS LIVE

Leopards once had a large **range**. They were found all over Africa, in parts of the Middle East, and in central and southern Asia. However, their range has shrunk over time. While Asia is still home to some leopards, most of the leopards living today are found in Africa. This makes Africa an ideal place to track these big cats.

This leopard is in the African country of Namibia. Leopards can be found in many Namibian habitats, including deserts, grasslands, and woodlands.

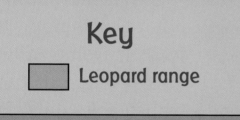

Map of Leopards in Africa

Atlantic
Ocean

Indian
Ocean

Key

☐ Leopard range

Leopards are adaptable. They can live in a number of habitats. Some live in grasslands or woodlands. Others live in tropical rain forests. Leopards like to live in places that have trees they can climb. However, they do not need to live near drinking water. They get enough water from the food they eat.

SEEING SPOTS

Leopards have great **camouflage**. Their spots let them blend in with the light and shadows around them. This lets them hide in plain sight from their **prey**. Leopards that live in bright grasslands have lighter-colored coats than those that live in dark rain forests. Some rain-forest leopards have all-black coats. Even trackers find it hard to spot leopards. This is one reason they rely on poop and other signs to find leopards.

All-black leopards, such as this one, are often known as black panthers.

Animals with solid coats tend to stand out more than animals with markings do. A leopard's rosettes actually make it less noticeable.

The spots on leopards' backs are called rosettes. They are generally tan or beige in the middle. The tips of leopards' tails and ears are white. This helps leopards **communicate** with each other in tall grass.

IN LEOPARD TERRITORY

As adults, leopards are solitary. This means they spend their time alone instead of living in groups. Most leopards are **nocturnal**. During the day, they rest. At night, they wake up to hunt and patrol their territories. Male leopards make a barking call that tells other leopards to stay out.

Leopards often rest in trees. They are excellent climbers.

Trackers look for the scratch marks that leopards leave on their favorite scratching trees. These are signs that a leopard is likely to be nearby.

Leopards mark their territories to keep other leopards away. They spray urine, or pee, around their territories. They also leave scat on the paths where they travel. Leopards scratch and rub themselves against trees. Scratching and rubbing leave scent marks that tell other leopards they are in another leopard's territory.

LOOK, IT'S A CUB!

Leopards can **mate** all year round. A female leopard calls out to nearby males when she is ready to mate. About 100 days later, she will have a **litter** of two or three babies, called cubs.

Mother leopards hide newborn cubs in logs, thick bushes, caves, or burrows while they are out hunting. Though good trackers can spot these, they know not to get too close. Mothers will attack people to defend their cubs. After a few months, cubs are big enough to follow their mothers around. Cubs live with their mothers for up to two years. Then, they find their own territories.

As they grow, leopard cubs chase and play with their mother. This teaches them how to chase and hunt prey. They also learn to climb trees and swim.

HUNTING PREY

Leopards hunt at night. Their good vision and hearing let them find prey in the dark. Leopards do not chase prey for long distances. Instead, they quietly **stalk** their prey until they get close to it. Then, they jump out and swat at it. Leopards' sharp claws help them grab their prey. Leopards kill prey by biting their necks.

This leopard is stalking prey. You can see how its color and rosettes help camouflage the leopard as it crouches amid grasses and rocks.

This leopard has pulled the carcass, or body, of an antelope it killed up into a tree. When trackers spot carcasses in trees, they know that a leopard is nearby.

Leopards are known for dragging their food up into trees. A leopard can climb 50 feet (15 m) high into a tree carrying a dead animal in its mouth. Bringing their food into trees keeps other animals from stealing it.

WHAT LEOPARDS EAT

Leopards are **carnivores**, meaning they eat only meat. Leopards will hunt any animal they can find in their habitat. This includes monkeys, snakes, antelopes, and rodents. Leopards even hunt cheetah cubs. Leopards are very good swimmers and sometimes go fishing.

LEOPARD DISGESTIVE SYSTEM

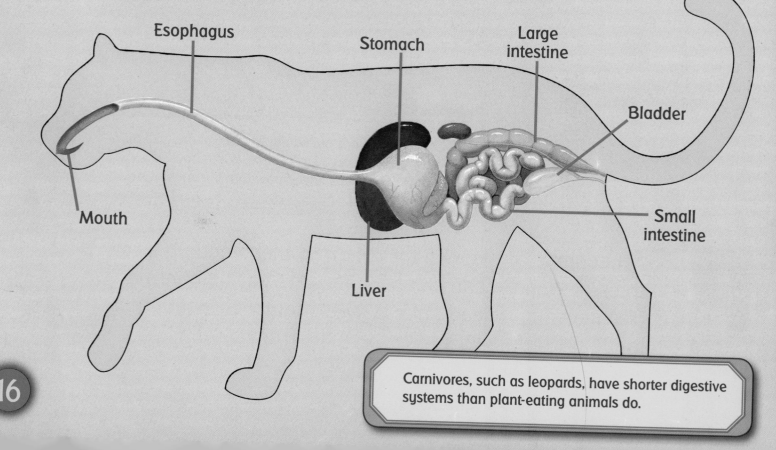

Esophagus

Stomach

Large intestine

Bladder

Mouth

Liver

Small intestine

Carnivores, such as leopards, have shorter digestive systems than plant-eating animals do.

The food a leopard eats enters its digestive system. There, it is broken down to provide the energy the leopard needs. Poop and urine are the waste from this process.

The bones and fur of a leopard's prey can be seen in its poop. Leopard poop is segmented, meaning it is made up of connected pieces. It is generally about .75 to 1.5 inches (2–4 cm) thick. Leopard poop looks similar to lion poop, but it is smaller. Sometimes several leopards' poops can be found where their paths cross.

TRACKING METHODS

You can learn a lot from leopard poop. For example, you can figure out what a leopard has been eating or if it is sick by looking at its poop. Both safari trackers and scientists use poop to learn about leopards.

People also use leopard tracks to find leopards. Leopards' claws are retractable, or able to be pulled back into their paws. This is why their tracks rarely have claw marks.

3–4 inches (8–10 cm) long

No claw marks

Four toes

LEOPARD TRACKS

KINDS OF LEOPARD POOP

Basic poop: Segmented and dark, with bits of hair and bone. Tends to be 1 to 2 inches (2.5–5 cm) wide.

Hairy poop: Poop from a leopard that fed on whole animals, not just meat. Often includes chunks of bone, too.

Runny poop: Very fresh poop from a leopard that was eating mainly meat.

White poop: Older poop that has been in the sun for several days and has calcium from animal bones in it.

Leopard poop contains DNA. Scientists can use this to tell the poop from different leopards apart. This helps scientists tell how many leopards live in an area. Scientists also capture leopards and put radio collars on them. The collars help scientists track the leopard's movements. Scientists also use camera traps that take photos of leopards whenever they pass by.

Today, many leopards live in national parks and **reserves**. For example, visitors can see leopards at the Sabi Sands Private Game Reserve, in South Africa. Places like this often have safari trackers, who find animals for visitors to observe. These trackers often rely on animal poop to find animals.

National parks and game reserves help keep leopards safe. In many leopard habitats, trees have been cut down for building or farming. **Poachers** kill leopards for their coats and whiskers. Leopards that live close to people are often poisoned. This is because leopards sometimes kill farmers' livestock. Leopards have also attacked people, though this is quite rare.

This leopard is in the Maasai Mara Game Reserve, in Kenya. Leopards are just one of many animals trackers can see there.

KEEPING LEOPARDS SAFE

Each year, we learn more about leopards' lives by tracking them. Tracking leopards also helps keep leopards safe by showing where they are. Knowing where leopards are can help wildlife groups protect them from poachers.

People must work together to keep leopards from dying out. One way to do this is to protect leopard habitats. This makes sure leopards have a safe place to live and enough food to eat. Getting involved with wildlife groups is a great way to help keep leopards safe!

Leopards, like this one at South Africa's Sabi Sands Private Game Reserve, visit water holes to try to find prey. Their poop can tell us what kinds of prey they find there.

GLOSSARY

camouflage (KA-muh-flahj) A color or shape that matches what is around something and helps hide it.

carnivores (KAHR-neh-vorz) Animals that eat only other animals.

communicate (kuh-MYOO-nih-kayt) To share facts or feelings.

habitats (HA-buh-tats) The kinds of land where animals or plants naturally live.

litter (LIH-ter) A group of babies born to the same mother at the same time.

mate (MAYT) To come together to make babies.

nocturnal (nok-TUR-nul) Active during the night.

poachers (POH-cherz) People who illegally kill animals that are protected by the law.

prey (PRAY) An animal that is hunted by another animal for food.

range (RAYNJ) The places in which a kind of animal can be found.

reserves (rih-ZURVZ) Land set aside for wildlife.

stalk (STOK) To follow something closely and secretly.

territories (TER-uh-tor-eez) Land or space that animals guard for their use.

INDEX

A
Africa, 4, 6
Asia, 4, 6

B
branches, 4

C
camouflage, 8
carnivores, 16
cats, 4, 6

G
grass(es), 4, 9
grasslands, 7–8

H
habitat(s), 4, 7, 16,
  20, 22

L
litter, 12

M
Middle East, 6
mother(s), 12

P
people, 5, 12, 20, 22
poachers, 20, 22
prey, 8, 14, 17

R
range, 6
reserve(s), 20

S
scat, 5, 11
spots, 4, 8–9, 12

T
territories, 5, 10–12

W
wild, 4
woodlands, 7

WEBSITES

For web resources related to the subject of this book, go to:
www.windmillbooks.com/weblinks and select this book's title.